SHAHID READS HIS OWN PALM

Shahid Reads His Own Palm

Reginald Dwayne Betts

ALICE JAMES BOOKS | FARMINGTON, MAINE

10 9 8 7 6 5 4 3 2 1

Alice James Books are published by Alice James Poetry Cooperative, Inc.,
an affiliate of the University of Maine at Farmington.

ALICE JAMES BOOKS
238 MAIN STREET
FARMINGTON, ME 04938

www.alicejamesbooks.org

Library of Congress Cataloging-in-Publication Data

Betts, Reginald Dwayne, 1980–
Shahid reads his own palm / Reginald Dwayne Betts.
    p. cm.
ISBN 978-1-882295-81-4
I. Title.
PS3602.E826S53 2010   2010000114

Alice James Books gratefully acknowledges support from individual
donors, private foundations, the University of Maine at Farmington
and the National Endowment for the Arts.

Cover art: Victor Ehikhamenor, *Labyrinths of a Palm Reader's Dreams*

ACKNOWLEDGMENTS

Thanks to the editors of the following journals in which these poems, at times in different versions, first appeared or are forthcoming:

Ploughshares: "Ghazal" (In Prison)
Puerto del Sol: "Near Nightfall"
Crab Orchard Review: "Shahid Reads His Own Palm"
Pebble Lake Review: "The Spanish Word for Solitude"
Nimrod: "How to Make a Knife in Prison"
Ninth Letter: "Dear Isaac," appeared in an altered version
     as "Dear Kareem,"
Gulf Coast: "Red Onion State Prison"
Connotation Press: An Online Artifact: "Sometimes It's Everything"
     and "A Father Talks to Himself"
Indiana Review: "Count Time"
Pluck: "Ghazal" (Breath)
Poet Lore: "Winter Hunger"
The Collagist: "Dear Augusta," and "Love in the Time of Chain-link
     Fences"

A version of "Your Mother's Questions" appeared in Fingernails Across the Chalkboard, edited by Randal Horton, M. L. Hunter and Becky Thompson, published by Third World Press, 2007.

THIS BOOK HAS a long list of people who ushered it out of my head and onto the page. Thanks to everyone I met inside the walls of the Fairfax County Jail, Southampton Correctional Center, Red Onion State Prison, Sussex 1 State Prison, Augusta Correctional Center, and Coffeewood Correctional Center, to everyone who has lived through the burden of a state number. Thanks to Randall Horton, John Murillo, and Remica Bingham, the first folks to read these pages and help me make a handful of words a book. The title poem of this collection comes from an exercise I did with Elizabeth Alexander, my first year at Cave Canem. Thanks to Elizabeth for making me think about what a long line I come from. Thanks to TSE for encouraging me to write a poem that moves in the world like I do. To Toi Derricotte, Cornelius Eady and every poet who has ever been touched by Cave Canem. Thanks to Marita Golden, Clyde McElvene and the Hurston/Wright Foundation. To the Fine Arts Work Center, the Bread Loaf Writers' Conference, the University of Maryland, and Warren Wilson College, all places that let me grow. Thanks to Michael Collier and Josh Weiner. Thanks to Reginald Gibbons, who helped me carve my sounds into a voice. Thanks to Ellen Bryant Voigt, Gabrielle Calvocoressi, and Heather McHugh. Thanks to Alice James Books for making this happen. To Catherine Barnett for taking a close look. To Lacy Simons, Julia Bouwsma, and Carey Salerno for making Alice James my home and believing in my project. To everyone who has cared to believe me when I called myself poet. To Tony Hoagland, for responding to a letter written from a young man aspiring to be a poet despite handcuffs. To Ethelbert Miller for always asking me if I've spoken with my dad.

To the memory of my Grandma Betts, who encouraged my shout even when it was from behind steel bars. To the memory of Dr. Corrie Haines, I've never forgotten what you told me.

Special thanks to my Moms, who wrote the first poem I ever read.

And for my wife Terese and our son, Micah, who both give me reason to add to the songs I sing.

CONTENTS

Ghazal

Who knows the blues of life in prison?
A man handcuffed to life in prison.

They know those cells plait his hair with fear—
will it make him a wife in prison?

Shahid's time far outweighs his secret.
So what he has a knife in prison.

Shahid Reads His Own Palm

I come from the cracked hands of men who used
        the smoldering ends of blunts to blow shotguns,

men who arranged their lives around the mystery
        of the moon breaking a street corner in half.

I come from "Swann Road" written in a child's
        slanted block letters across a playground fence,

the orange globe with black stripes in Bishop's left
        hand, untethered and rolling to the sideline,

a crowd openmouthed, waiting to see the end
        of the sweetest crossover in a Virginia state pen.

I come from Friday night's humid and musty air,
        Junk Yard Band cranking in a stolen Bonneville,

a tilted bottle of Wild Irish Rose against my lips
        and King Hedley's secret written in the lines of my palm.

I come from beneath a cloud of white smoke, a lit pipe
        and the way glass heats rocks into a piece of heaven,

from the weight of nothing in my palm,
        a bullet in an unfired snub-nosed revolver.

And every day the small muscles in my finger threaten to pull
        a trigger, slight and curved like my woman's eyelashes.

Near Nightfall

The phone ringing stops everything and the cold voice
draws a body in white chalk—
says your son has been at the precinct since last night.

Before you leave the house, you've smoked four cigarettes
and as you drive, smoke
drifts into your eyes.
The house lights were already on and his bedroom door

a sliver of light that crossed you
when
your foot pushed it open. His absence was a question:
the Newports left unopened in your purse for years. For a moment

you almost expected to find him,
his voice barely above a whisper. The television
hummed;
it made the door an invite—but he is gone,

and you see yesterday's clothes on the floor,
books, video games and sneakers
on the bed, under the bed. He is not on the bed,

phone to his ear as usual—the door is still open.
It's Sunday and there's
no reason for his absence. Against the shadows,
hints of your laughter:

his first word was "no,"
a picture with Orioles cap on big enough
for his father,
and his face etched with red tracings of Kool-Aid.

He needs to know
you expected him home, and why smoke from a Newport
leaves the taste of metal
in your mouth.

The Spanish Word for Solitude

Soledad is a mouth
        full of dust, the taste
of Guinness & one night

a trigger tucked under
        my index like a
spliff. It is a man

awakened by a .380's
        muzzle, or
my heart folded

into a cell. Soledad is
        the six fingers
I need to number

my felonies,
        the bright orange
of my county

jumpsuit, my
        shackled feet, the
chain-link belt

around my waist
        & yesterdays yoked
into my cuffed hands.

Two Nightmares

By moonglow, by the way silver
flits from there to here, from past
where our eyes can see to here
where we want to hide our eyes
& behind the lit end of a cigarette,
the tobacco spark dusting
the air with smoke, a man slumps
into the door he can't open. Every
door is a door to somewhere &
all the strength in his back wants
to get him somewhere else, away
from the clank of a tray slot
signaling chow time. His name is
another tedium, a door to the night
that birthed this mad riot of cuffs
and apologies, the night a gun
on safety made a man forget
his first name. Fear is a beast.
& look now: two men tied
to doors, one the unnamed can't
open, the other a door the
one called victim can't close.

How to Make a Knife in Prison

The rec yard brims
with 219 shades
of brown & Sam leans
like a stolen hubcap
against a bend
in the fence. He works
a section over,
pushes and pulls
at a curve until a ten-
inch slat falls
into his palms &
he tucks the slab
near his crotch
& starts chasing
silhouettes of ex-lovers
around a quarter mile
track, his nostrils
clouded with the sweat
of men. Lockdown

brings him to his knees.
His hand palms
the scrap like a priest
about to carve
a god. He sprinkles
water near his feet
to keep the blade
from folding, slides
his arms across
concrete. In his head,
a man holds
the bit of stomach

beneath belt
and bleeds. The hands
remember this
as he works
the fence
piece into
enough.

Sometimes It's Everything

Time & what else moves man to shape scrap
        metal into God's tongue? Call it a bid:
slang for a stretch, a mandatory minimum that leaves
        years swollen into the thirty seconds
it took to kill & reasons are worthless once
        cuffs close wrists after a night's dirt turns

into a war story for the body left owned by
        a cell's straight lines & right angles. & no one
cares for nothing, not about parole chances
        wrapped in time's chastity belt, or secrets
cockeyed soap-dice tell when they stop dead on
        snakes, or why the block is always still,

a casket of seconds, echoes, fists or nothing. Chants.

And What if Every Cuss Word Was a Sin

Mouths would blossom more
thorns & men—shackled to bunk
beds, chow calls and count times,
their tongues touching pain
so rich it crawled inside bruises
and began to beat,—still wouldn't
give a fuck if God was listening.
Everything halved by hurt. & shit
would be so real, prayers would come
as cut cards saved & muthafuckas
stitched inside the soles of prison
brogans, coats padded with magazines
and the edges of ice picks
or flat blades of carved steel. Mercy
would be the nine of hearts turning
the book that leaves your footlocker
full, silence the craving when you
want a woman's touch but your dick
is in your hand & men would list
the pain all in swears, confusing the meaning,
until each shit, bitch & muthafucka
was solemn: our heads bowed in abeyance.

In the Yard, Facing the Fences

Scars tap dance & moonwalk,
smashed beneath drying ink
& look, fifty-two years casket
your dreams in shackles

& since Pops Smith got his
parole papers, these doors should
swing slantways for everybody

& behind me seven men
in a circle call each other god &
the banger is in the cut, is buried in the dirt

(the banger is speed is omen is weapon is truth is ice pick is sharp is
steel is prayer is death is smoke is there is waiting is carved is light is
circular is flat is nothing is need is hurt is cold is blood is warm is is)

& is nothing.
Forty-four cells, bruised eyes open
staring at the C/O, shot-

gun clutched, the buckshot
still on the floor from last week
when Pimp got a patch on his eye;

& the fence steel is slimmer
than a Newport & these eyes
watering, thinking who gives a fuck
about birds, sinking like quicksand.

Ghazal

In the hole, guards dream me below the sky above—
disturbed, they watch me. I shadow the sky above.

My cellmate calls prison the devil's echo.
I show him god's first flambeau: the sky above.

Justin swears he wants to defy gravity,
and fall up 'til he swallows the sky above.

The Judge parted time with a ridged machete,
and left nightmares to bestow the sky above.

After it rained, she asked for a carmine shroud.
He used purple thread to sew the sky above.

He wanted the world opened up with one answer.
Where rests the world's true sorrow? The sky above.

He asked to "hold a dollar 'til tomorrow."
He should have asked to borrow the sky above.

Should I gift to my lover this mouth of lies?
No, this will delight my beau: the sky above.

Shahid's fingers were left in a cotton field—
now he forever cornrows the sky above.

Supreme Mathematics

Trigger and Wise wrap
hands hidden in socks
over a steel bar
and tug their weight.

Their upper bodies bear
painted flags: the miracle
of a prison tattoo gun,
ink stolen from smoke.

Cold air pushes hard
out their mouths.
They count off reps.
When they pull, the splash

of colors against their skin
splices the air. Each rep
could be a year in prison,
and after two hours

Wise would still be
counting, the sound
of numbers snuffing
out everything else.

Fantasy Girl

Ripped from Black Tail's pages,
her open legs twisted into
a pair of crescent moons, beckoning
above screams hissed from a mouth full
of piss-soaked sock. Heather stares
at me from Jeremy's angled back. Everything

in this cell is mine. This knife-slim
boy beneath me, bought with my last
pack of blows; my pencil thin ice
pick hinting silver in my clenched fist.
His body falls limp in my arms

and it doesn't matter. I will
finish, peel Heather from his back
and lay him in bed. He clamps
his eyes shut. I pretend he's
quivering, pleased.

It Takes the Bus Four Hours to Get There

Dirt & rocks wedged between the
        soles of his state boots,
still black and scuffed from wear,
        Stephen posts up, that is stands,
a busted out light bulb in the middle of the city.
        He waits for Aunt Thelma as a thousand

bricks shaped into a casket
        of apologies hold men & their promises
before the sound of a fired pistol folds
        them into nothing more
than a list of bodies lined up in hallways
        & behind eyelids & shuts off everything, until

Aunt Thelma's eyes show
        crooked details left propped against her
memory: Stephan's hand carrying a pistol
        & statistics that walked her towards a
visiting room & closed her son off in a funk.

What Your Mother Asks, and What I Never Say

Have you ever had sex with a man?
Were you raped? Abused in someway?

You want details, the camera to pan.
Have you ever had sex with a man?

You want the lens to focus and span
umbrae. You wonder if I sashayed.

Have you ever had sex with a man?
Were you raped? Abused in someway?

A Head Full of Feathers

There is a drowned man who
will tell everything, his head
buried in a sentence, his head full
of feathers and nothing, of flowers
and fists, the broken backs men hide
with bed covers, the lies wrapped
in dust balls, and what happens when
no one is looking.
In the middle of the silence, before
he speaks, is your chance. Walk away.
There is nothing good in his words:
only stories of what happens
when men have power in the dark.

A Father Talks to Himself

A fist tonight: slams upside my head,
       brushes wind, which brushes yesterday's
              potash off my shirt. I dug dirt for hours

and planted St. Augustine grass on land
       still begging water's touch. I say fuck this
              starved ground, this rain, the crimes that lend my face

to Junior's wild, wild life. I know some things.
       It's April now, with the sun cutting shadows
              into dead men on grass and gravel, when

my arm transforms this shovel into a shank that jabs
       at earth, my fist holding the spade's thin neck.
              I know the size of the cell Junior calls home

and how it talks to him at night, each night.
       It was built with bricks the same as Lorton's hell,
              that hardened mud that draws out hurt from bones

and pulls what's left into a fist. I called
       my sister asking where my son had gone.
              A man is crushed when he doesn't know steps

that will lead back to the years and life he left
       behind for a fight with the streets and night's hunger.
              His mom don't call my name for nothing since

she left its sound in my mad machete rage;
       she left my voice in a cage and I don't blame
              that woman for love. I never was enough

saint to leave sin with the devil, leave my lies
        unsaid. I lived flush with the anger that ran
                my son to jail. Never did teach him much

about the land, or how this rain is good
        for any grass. Now I swallow regrets.
                Let the rain learn me something about hurt.

Love in the Time of Chain-link Fences

I watched. There was a chain-link fence, a
tear falling from her face. The echo of a car
door slamming. It was Saturday. Believe me
when I tell you I fell in love. Not with her, but
with her tears. It was a Saturday & the sun
was a fat globe in the sky. I'd been staring
at it, trying to fix my eyes, when she pulled
into the parking lot. The driver's side door
slammed my fantasies into a question mark.
Dave's sister. She visited twice a month. Her
hair the color of the back of my hand. I dreamed
about her for weeks & wrote her letters.
She cried when she walked to the car an hour
after walking in, ashamed at her brother in
chains. I wanted her to be ashamed of me.

Dear Augusta,

        Your walls never surrender,
call out names, or
recognize the sound of bodies
thumping against years as a mother's
slatted prayer. If you mourn for the innocent,

straightjacket swaddled in a padded
room, mourn, too, for the young
man, a jackal screaming inside his head.
Augusta, you know Marquette
and how years multiplied
as tattoos along his arms, along
his back, and how a judge declared
the parking lot will fill with trees

before he breathes again.
You know Quincy,
namesake of the man who first sold
his mother a casket of dreams
under a buck-knifed moon. You know
Los, Adrian, Tariq.
One afternoon Rashad
broke the collar of midnight,
streaks of a Norfolk street
running down
his face.

Ahmad called his cell home,
called it his hut. Your
walls became the breastbone
he laid his head upon, the darkness
behind his eyelids. Under

a weather-worn staircase, he
shaped the handle of a plunger
into a reason for men cowed
by screams to look another
direction, to seek out the wind.

Dear Augusta, what do
names mean? You
know Universal, Moe-Moe,
Jake—all juveniles when they grilled
the camera for a photo ID, when you
gave them this language
of survival and blood.

Red Onion State Prison

A warehouse of iron
bunks: straight lines
& right angles

flush against the gutted
side of a mountain.
Inside, white paint

cracks into a thousand
pockmarks and listens
to the sound of a padlock

splitting a man's scalp &
voices of guards in shot-
guns or the hand that tilts

a slender metal rod,
then scrapes it against
concrete & stretches night

longer than a sinner's
prayer in Red Onion's small
ruined cells where ten thousand

years of sentences
beckon over heads & hearts,
silent, a promise, like mistletoe.

Tell This to the People You Love

or think about—the young boy,
          whose name you won't say,
name written in dirt by
          the fence,
                    on walls, benches
'cause
          prison cells drive men to practice
history, writing names—their own,
someone else's—into
          more than the moment
          his body flattened air, a snow
angel for a second, as he
          leaped from the top tier,
from a half dozen war stories & cuffs
                              on wrists: memory, anecdote & under
          that is what a life
sentence does to men, or
          a five-year sentence, any
stretch, bid, length of time where
          time leads to nowhere but
another cell & the
          boy whose name
          you won't tell was
                    hemmed up inside
          this corner cell where the
horror of everything cuts at
          what's left of his world,
retrospect & this:
          the name you'll write for
                    mad days in

your sleep but won't let fall,

                    the things you heard:
stray cats that ran wild here
              & still cry at night, all
straining against what's thrown at them.

Mariposa

This is the thing: there is nothing to say
                              about Dave. He cut a T-shirt in half &
tied what was left into a knot around his
                              waist. It gave him Sandra's legs, bowed
into the wish she inspired in men
                              before she began talking to God through
smoke & a glass pipe. Cats started calling
                              him redbone. He wanted us
to call him Vanessa & curled his hair
                              with the steam men used to cook
noodles. Some places you can't run away from.
                              But I'm not talking about those places.
I'm talking about Dave & how at night he stared
                              into the mirror & waited for two
things: he wanted a cocoon to crawl inside;
                              he wanted wings he was promised
when Jose called him his *mariposa*.

When Mathematics Has Nothing to Do with Counting

"Do the *math*" & half
        the brown faces have
no clue what the *math* is—

young boys: nothing but teeth
        & ten chins pressed
against the cell's grill,

but that's enough
        to build a world
around. "Do

the *science*. Do the
        knowledge." & Divine
Allah's voice—a

child, too, for real—
        talks from behind
scraps of Elijah

Muhammad's legacy
        tatted into meaning:
sevens & *five-*

pointed stars birthed
        by bids & cell
doors. These boys

listening have no
        more need
to count. Time

has turned knowledge
        trivial:
the population

of the earth,
        the weight of the brain,
a moment, a word—

        everything at some
point loses meaning.

The Day Carlos Jumped from the Top Tier

A bloodied white shirt, the body of a life
Sentence half hidden by the icebox. Everything
Darkens. A dozen or so wild eyes over
It. Steam from the shower over it. Rehabilitation
A lit Newport. This is what we talk about.
The body below the tier, the small gasps
Without a story, with no words for this story.
It is a man. He is someone's son. A heartsore.
When he screams, our eyes open. Again.
A bid's honesty: time staring at time.
Whatever smell is there lies low, won't step
Up. A sock kicks out & the sigh that follows
Follows a stray cat's yowl. It is always raining.
From the outside, everything in here inspires
Screams. If you stand on the top tier, the drop
Is from hell to hell. It is many falls. Someone
Pretends to know something worth knowing.
The body is fifteen feet past knowledge. People
Say he bodied himself. Stretched himself out.
If he rises, who will he turn to? Or turn into?

Ode to a Kite

& they rename you kite, as if a word can make wings.
You are a piece of paper tied to string, singing like a schoolgirl.
The paper flung into the hall & spit into another cell

or folded neatly into an envelope & dropped into a mailbox.
The envelope always has a rose drawn on the corner. Sweet weight,
your nothingness is the kind of hope that keeps razors

from plucking away at the flesh covering a vein. Tell them you're
not worthy. Whisper everything you hold back into their ears
as ink seeps into the white of you.

If the arm pressed on the table was yours, you'd want the truth about
flight. Tell those men a letter is just a letter, let them know that a name
alone can never grant wings. & still say you love it: to be called kite. Yes.

In Meathead's Smile

A missing day is a story told by God
about something worse
than five young men flexing

in fresh white tees. They pose before
the commissary and none of them thinks
the name Snake or Pooh suggests bars

clanking behind them at night; even
Double Barrel started as nothing
but the explanation for Darnel Thomas's

refusal to pass the ball. In Meathead's smile
you can't find one of the fifty-four years
bloody hands and a broken street in Richmond

left him. Men know this as they rustle
together and pull back sleeves to show
tattoos smeared by Vaseline and blood.

Shahid Riffs on Ancestors

Hennessy & backwash splash
the trash can & I bless
Swann Rd. and the air below my spit
with whatever's left
in my glass,
leaning on how crime split
lives into silence, how
words & wildness are still
buried after an hour
of cognac filling my brain
with lighter fluid, breaking
open the truth of why
when I hear talk of ancestors
it's never Mario
who took what he knows
with him, afternoons he
held down the block & the wind
talked with his audacity. Ancestors
are only the folks you know
who earned (or stole) a bus pass to
Heaven.
So don't go looking for them
in Mama's laughs
or Keisha's slanted
eyelashes, not under
clouds or in the hoofbeats of
a train. Ain't know? The
bridge linking them
to you is a dance
you haven't mastered,
stories of men who broke nights
into fistfuls of money
& smoke, men

yoked to somebody
else's dream, maybe. But
then again maybe not—
maybe the glass
& liquor I throw
against the trash can
isn't a symbol.
Maybe it's just glass
that smashes
like rose petals
dropped into the shape
of a compass over a grave.

Dear Isaac,

                I once told a story about you & about
a picture in your cell—
you and Tiffany, the third prettiest

girl in the eighth grade before
you owned that dead man. I said you
wanted that day back, when living

was a chance to kiss a pretty girl. I made
it all up: there was no girl, no reminder
of the life you left.

Fuck everything you've ever heard
about survival. I've never seen your cell.
All I know is *count time*

is the same everywhere & that we
all get buried when balancing life
on a blade's edge.

Ghazal

Some lies multiply and then blunt breath—
or they flair out into hot, brilliant breath.

What secret died with the jail's shorn locks?
How to unlock woman's silent breath.

So many black men, brown men in prison,
is there a name for such migrant breath?

Kicks has spent three decades in prison,
who writes stories with his absent breath?

Dream Weaver, my lover spurns my kiss—
she walks away, takes a giant breath.

Cry. Slowly with the force of whispers,
and let it strut with strong elephant breath.

Banger, speed, shank, steel, ice pick, razor—
jail slang for knife, for violent breath?

O Judge, I have swallowed silences, silences,
on your ear I blow my lucent breath.

Sentenced to life in prison. Life. In prison.
What judge declares more to shunt breath?

Shahid waits, listens to the stars—
His mind is a cell: blow through it ancient breath.

Juvenile's Letter

This is the story of
        dice-turned
out-cupped hands falling
        onto the scuffed
concrete floor,

      of me
one morning with
        a lawnmower blade in
my hand trying to
        shank a prison

to death, of
        Sussex 1 State Prison,
a half-empty
        reason for a few men to
walk with their heads

        down, a working man's
hat tilted into
        a razor cutting
at my parole chances,
        of the barbershop

where my hair got
        cropped close like
my daddy's, of men who
        told me how 'Nam left
needles to fill

their hunger,
        of my back curved, fish-
hooked to nights when

I would have told
        God I owned the wind
& Richmond, of screams
        in my ears now, of how the hours
not teaching my son to

        tie his shoes are pushing
my hands holding
        a two-inch long plastic
        pen over this table
hitched to the wall by
        deadbolts & a decade of
dust—
        if you want
the logic of birthdays

        and anniversaries, turn
your face away
        from what I write
now with this
        scribble that cuts paper

into a million
        broken syringes,
the weight
        of my arm sure
as the night's count

        bell on this table,
sure as the no
        I got from the parole
board, my eighth turn-
        down 'cause the

board thinks thirteen
        years in a box isn't

enough to turn the
        wildness in a man
whose father never voted

        into anything
but more rage, but a brush
        fire waiting to happen &
memories, those lies
        that fold my body

into a half-
        moon wrapped around
this desk & threaten to drown
what refuses to listen.

The Sound of My Mother Crying

The first step to confessing is to walk into a parking
lot with a pistol. A .380 because it disappears in your palm
like loaded dice. There were strands of a song cupped
in my hands that night & I want to remember.
The man before me wore a white shirt he'd worn
too many times. The light was jail cell light & reflected
a morning I wish hadn't awakened me. Parole
had been dumped for truth in sentencing & GM
had laid off half the people in a city I've never visited.
There is a secret in all of this & so everything I denied
could still be denied, taken back. A head fake, if you will.
The tape recorder spoke to me, read back my words. But
listen, the man in his car wasn't as much asleep as
waiting for something in his life to happen. To move
him from where he was to where he could go &
there are people I know who have died waiting to be.
I opened his hurt. I pushed the eye of the gun under
his ear & thought of what angle his shock against
my fear formed. I taunted him, maybe. Asked if he
was a cop. There is a song, "Life Goes On," that ends
in a life sentence. Imagine this: I scribbled
my name on the confession. You tell your mother that.
Tell her you admitted that the gun was
a kiss & it was so close to the forehead of the sleeping
man that if you were his woman he would have moaned.

An Opened Vein

Straight up, the curve of a wrist is beautiful,
majestic, another reason to open your heart.

& if this is ridiculous to you, I understand.
There is a day that none of us knows
anything about & it could be a Thursday

& this is all the reason you need. Before
you, barbed wire coiled into a wish;
a fence is coiled into a thousand wrists,

hands fallen on the other side of prison,
where freedom is a body still searching

for the rest of itself. If you've seen this day,
you know what it feels like to have a razor blade
in the meaty side of your jaw—there are ways

a man is tortured that only he can tell you.
Listen, hurt opens the world

and makes you want
to climb into the curve of your own wrist,
lay your burden down against

the line that leads to your thumb.
There's a lesson in this somewhere. The razor on

your pulse, digging in. The flesh,
I swear, you can taste it, the crimson,
& your eyes will run over.

Saturdays Waited

for bodies
        visiting from
outside, walking

into centers
        of correction,
to get strip

searched, reminded
of how a word—

C/O, kite, ice
        pick, death
row—tossed

into a room
        of men
changes everything.

On the other
        side, there
is a man &

a balled
        fist, quiet
while guards'

hands
        rummage
boots, a white

shirt, boxers—
        as if there
exists something

anyone would
        bring from
a prison cell

        to his younger
brother; while
on the other

side, a bra strap
        reminds
a metal detector

of a knife, or
        reminds
a guard

of flesh: some-
        thing soft
walking, eyes

open, ready
        to still
even life-

sentence-bad
        men who
squat and cough

contempt, lift
        bared feet, wait
for a table,

pray for
        visitors, hands
always cold

& reaching,
        empty, so
empty. Aware.

After Midnight

On shadows that turn
        the wall into
yesterday, behind
        black the sheet
touches once
        it folds over
night and splits
        the wall in
half, when a man washes
        his hands over
a sink, there, just
        above the toilet, its
gray steel almost
        invisible at the
darkest hour of
        night, the moon
spits the flat
        side of a blade
onto the wall
        where the naked
woman hangs
        below dinks
that form mistle-
        toe & on top
of three words
        scratched into
concrete that read
        Slim was here.

Count Time

& so what you want it to be
more than what it is—
the flashlights dotting dark-
ness, their yellow calling
you a liar, saying fifteen
counts a day is routine,
not the system's rhetoric
calling you linear: 3,285 days
where you will stand
once every eight hours
to the creaking
of bunks, sheets knotted
at the ends & hanging
toward the floor, state
boots scraping the ground
& no one knows if
you're hanging or if you're
standing & every minute
you spend knees bent,
hand holding a white cloth
wet with wax, turning
a corner cell into a
corner cell, until you see
your reflection in glass, is
a sign, something a friend
could read in the way
smoke pauses before running
from gravity, a ragged
reminder of a man somewhere,
or woman, whose job is to sit
at a desk and answer
letters about the black Xs
drawn through your days

& how there is another room,
somewhere, with another
man or woman, wearing
a hood, clutching a black
ink-pen, scratching
out your days (as if the days
are the crime) & they
do it until their rhythm is
the only one that matters.

One Grave

There is only one grave
near Red Onion, and Kevin swears

he saw a crow, a single
black crow dig one hole there.
He says nothing else
matters if you live a spit

away from a graveyard
and know you can only touch
that dirt if you die.

At least two people died
in the echoes of these walls,
but if you wanted

to count the maimed,
you'd need a list far
longer than a lifer's bid. Yes, you
could list those numbers as if

they meant something
to a man rumbling with the way
his breath stalls after
prison mash and a failed GED.

There is a graveyard outside
the walls that folks call
Red Onion. A man buried there listens
to the moans that erupt,

wrestles
with dusk to be the last
to see the slanted eyes of
Abdullah alone

in a cell, kneeling before
his bunk when a guard approaches
flashlight in hand and stares

at the body in prayer, body grown

huge on the wall, back
so straight it's a headstone,
and the whole prison a grave.

Ghazal

Bootlegger, mashmaker, ankle chains,
let me earn scars, deserve awful chains.

Did they say faithful? Then let them come—
few will lie in streets to cradle chains.

So I asked: lend me your new suede shoes?
But why add music to mental chains?

They say he once earned his jailor's respect—
still, what man desires loyal chains?

Lucifer, spurned light that falls through clouds,
will you pray away your fragile chains?

The Singer wonders about true love—
no, he wonders about brittle chains.

My lover yearns for an angel's grace.
Lord, let me dress her in crystal chains.

Let us be clear, nothing outlasts death?
Not even the taste of shackles, chains.

Palm reader, what of scarlet letters?
Should I honor them, or tackle chains?

Did they say faithful? Then let them come—
few will lie in streets to cradle chains.

What if Shahid had no choice, or worse—
let's say he was born with sessile chains.

Exchanging Contraband

Say a prayer for Damon's out-
        stretched arm flung into the space
an open window leaves, five

fingers gripping the back end of
        a line he ripped from a sheet slept
on last night—ripped by teeth & desperation—

say something about the strays
        that run back and forth through
trees, buildings, and ten dreams,

that run under his father's face,
        dead on the arm that weighs less

than his wish for a release date,
        his wanting a way out of the bowl
of oatmeal his mind sifts

through—the line weighs less than this
        except for the boot scuffed & brown
at the other end, falling to the ground

to wait for Raymond or Charles
        or José, whoever is in a cell on the other
side to toss the line they hold that drops to

the ground with the weight of a shampoo
        bottle filled with water—say
a prayer in homage to the way the

boot lands on dry grass with a thud, with
        the echo of a woman carrying a small
small child in her arms, somewhere

between the space of the two buildings
        & God: C2, for inmates
in population, and C3, the hole, the hole

or solitary confinement or the last place
        Damon's mother knows her son breathed.
Just say something that pulls

at the hair, that craves light, craves what
        it means to be a cat running free in
a prison yard, hungering for scraps, talk

about the sheet-line, how, once flung,
        it falls beside a tuft of burned grass,
just over the white line that holds the other boot

or bottle to the dry grass (thrown from
        population) & seems out of place
there, waiting for its twin to fall over it—

then Damon & whoever else tug
        at both ends, with the only
hope being a straight line in the air.

Tell the people that when it catches
        & is pulled taut, tight like the belly
of the last woman you kissed,

it means something you can't
        explain. Tell us the texture
of the empty pillow case someone

has tied to the line, empty & tell
how it floats

one building to the next, and then is
filled with cupcakes,
a book, lighter, pack of smokes:

little things that have become
cracked stand-ins for freedom,
stand-ins for the sound of a cat, walking.

The Secret Art of Lifting Time

Add silver plates to a fifteen
           pound bar and curl,
build muscle that will turn
           arms to hammers.
Curl the time the judge sledged
           between that crooked
gap in your teeth; soon the wedge
           is a world pitched under

the calluses that form across
           the pads of your hands.
Do a set counted out in reps
           of ten, and then do it until
your biceps bulge
           with the promise
of an early release, until the weight
           is every reason you're two

felonies short of a life sentence.
           What parole board will untie
the knot your bicep punches
           into a second at a time? Still
the sweat beading along your scalp?
           The aching inside your bones: just
shudders a man's body won't release.
           And nothing you curl changes
the bitterness of that weight.

Song

Lopsided soap-dice, roll!
And bank against the grainy
      box, thud liked a cocked pistol,
so if I call you my lady,
every cat near knows what smooth be.

      As the men gathered 'round
caress your misshapen sides—
stop on snake-eyes, let them knuckle down
with the devil 'fore they see tithes
      given to a life sentence's guide.

What matters? A carton of blows
      stacked against the edge of an ice
pick? Near-crumbled dice, although
sweaty palms beg, bury your advice—
      let seven tumble from a cool palm thrice.

Then turn dust in the hot hand,
      the shared fate of all things rare.
Who of them won't disband?
      The remnants of soap in their hair,
      the sound of stilled dice, still there!

Texas: Wine Man Speaks

From juice
       to three

packs of blows
       in my hands

& you won't

care. My white
       cup full of

crushed autumn
       leaves will be

your friend,
for a night. You'll

sip then guzzle
       this drink,
a man's

sweat & anger
       distilled into

eleven ounces

       of rotgut will
make your tongue
       lift, poet.

A Cell Houses a One-sided War

This old man, with his hair tied
by the cracked walls of cell B8, swore
some jail cells house a one-sided war,
and some men lean shoulders on past highs.

The cracked walls of cell B8 swore
broken men peeled back tattoos to cry
and some lean shoulders on past highs
after, clank! then yoke followed closed door.

Broken men peeled back tattoos to cry,
touched dirt as some wild man's whore
after, clank! then yoke followed closed door.
Nobody whispered to guards that Black Tye

touched dirt as some wild man's whore.
Name who is hurt by what they deny.
Nobody whispered to guards that Black Tye
now shivers for no reason, his body a sore.

Name who is hurt by what they deny
in court. Someone not warned before
now shivers for no reason, his body a sore.
Who knows escape is reason enough to lie

in court. Someone not warned before,
that some jails house a one-sided war.
Who knows escape is reason enough to lie:
this old man, with his hair tied.

The Honorable Bryant F. Bruce Explains a Life Sentence

I don't have any illusion that the penitentiary
is going to help you.
& I doesn't mean "me," per se,

I means "the judge," or "the United States
of America." Either way your life is knuckling
up with the shadow of a country. Know, too,

that *have* is more of the bad math behind
Wall Street & Swann Rd.: a pocket full of stones or
get it the best way you know how;

a brief case of *illusion*, unreal, out the pocket:
a gift,
a complex, another way

to say gotcha, to tell this story of a five-second
sentence where I carve your life in two,

into a mandatory minimum
& the cold violence of a cell where *help* is a misnomer

& you lift everything & sing, stool pigeon
your status above the thirty seconds

it took you to palm the pistol and go to work,
to leave all of yourself *going*, as in traveling,
pushing, migrating to a statistic, to a prison

of black men, to the suburbs of the suburbs,
west of nowhere. Meet your cousin, your uncle,
your father. Believe *is* means always & never.

Gift:

As in then, when
        uncle won death
& left his pistol—
        dinked pearl handle,
sure trouble—& left
        my mind unraveled
by heaven's
        refusal to
tell me who knows
        reasons are worse

        than death. Me
& an open door,
        as if every door
hadn't opened
        to a room full
of fathers—the history
        of heat & street
corners we claimed
        we owned or

the scraps of
        paper we all
wrote apologies on,
        gifts of bells,
words that tapered off
        into days of cells,

into Terrence Johnson's
        bullet, gifting
the same sour science

that left uncle closed
in, death forgiving where

life wouldn't & all
        is echoes and tithing.

The Truth About Four Leaf Clovers

Shahid imagines luck
        buried in the search,
tucked into the

        minutes of staring
at a field of clover,
        like trying to dance

with the yellow butterfly
        above his daughter
Amaya's head in the picture

        she sent, or opening
the shoebox he keeps under
        his bunk and rereading

the three letters she's written
        him in five years
and he would admit Amaya

        is too young to know
the value of her name printed
        on an envelope in a box,

or why she only sees him
        on weekends and then
not too often—he would tell

        his own father, if
they talked, that it's absurd, crazy
        to want his daughter

to remember how she smiled
        when he tossed her
into the summer's breeze,

        and really Shahid knows
luck tastes like the back
        end of a life sentence:

it is a child coloring
        outside every line
of a picture to mail

        to her incarcerated father.
He would say Shahid
is #251534, and some days

        that number means more
than his name; he says,

imagine this picture:
        three gray hairs
on my chin, my hand

reaching into grass
        that means nothing.

Prison

Prison the sinner's bouquet, house of shredded & torn
       Dear John letters, upended grave of names, moon
       Black kiss of a pistol's flat side, time blueborn
& threaded into a curse, Lazarus of hustlers, the picayune
Spinning into beatdowns; breath of a thief stilled
       By fluorescent lights, a system of 40 blocks,
       Empty vials, a hand full of purple cranesbills,
Memories of crates suspended from stairs, tied in knots
Around street lamps, the hours of unending push-ups,
       Wheelbarrels & walking 20s, the daughters
        Chasing their father's shadows, sons that upset
The wind with their secrets, the paraphrase of fractured,
       Scarred wings flying through smoke, each wild hour
       Of lockdown, hunger time & the blackened flower.

Winter Hunger

Your father watches the flecks add up.
He says the wind-blown dead insects
against the window conjure ghosts:
tossed dice, the South, and his regrets.

You're driving north on roads that glow
with high beams searching night. You cuss
and think about the wheel's curved bone
pressed on your palms. The hard callus

burns and you curse the time—eight years
these towns on green billboards were home—
Greensville, Nottoway, Sussex. Names
of prisons, dark restless tombstones.

Words swallow air between you two
as a Newport lights the car's inside.
Your father has listened and now wants
to talk. He pauses to glare wild-eyed.

His voice is broken bottles, smoke,
flesh. He knows you burned his letters.
In the back, your younger brother sleeps
between your wife and child for hours.

Outside, a storm begins with rain.
Your father sips his third straight beer
and you remember prison's night.
He never mentions love's austere

and lonely offices. And now—
when your son wakes—what will you say
about fathers? What will you say
about a voice cuffed to mistakes?

Ghazal

Men bleed without insight in prison?
A hand on neck starts a fight in prison.

He held the night's air in his fist and screamed,
then sent word by scribbled kite in prison.

Steve's eyes broke open to the bluest black,
then he wore homemade tights in prison.

Marquette splintered, deranged, pigeon insane.
He learned there is never flight in prison.

You wouldn't use a rusted blade to pull
a wrist vein, but a man just might in prison.

We read *Midsummer Night's Dream* on the yard,
then Snoop said, "I am a sprite in prison."

Tim stared at lipstick on his forehead—
believed passion ignites in prison.

Evan celled with his father at Augusta,
some discovery – birthright in prison.

But, for real, why does any of it matter?
Some men never pray at night in prison.

Blame me. Write another poem, a sad psalm.
Shahid, sing for the gods, right in prison.

RECENT TITLES FROM ALICE JAMES BOOKS

How to Catch a Falling Knife, Daniel Johnson
Phantom Noise, Brian Turner
Father Dirt, Mihaela Moscaliuc
Pageant, Joanna Fuhrman
The Bitter Withy, Donald Revell
Winter Tenor, Kevin Goodan
Slamming Open the Door, Kathleen Sheeder Bonanno
Rough Cradle, Betsy Sholl
Shelter, Carey Salerno
The Next Country, Idra Novey
Begin Anywhere, Frank Giampietro
The Usable Field, Jane Mead
King Baby, Lia Purpura
The Temple Gate Called Beautiful, David Kirby
Door to a Noisy Room, Peter Waldor
Beloved Idea, Ann Killough
The World in Place of Itself, Bill Rasmovicz
Equivocal, Julie Carr
A Thief of Strings, Donald Revell
Take What You Want, Henrietta Goodman
The Glass Age, Cole Swensen
The Case Against Happiness, Jean-Paul Pecqueur
Ruin, Cynthia Cruz
Forth A Raven, Christina Davis
The Pitch, Tom Thompson
Landscapes I & II, Lesle Lewis
Here, Bullet, Brian Turner
The Far Mosque, Kazim Ali
Gloryland, Anne Marie Macari
Polar, Dobby Gibson
Pennyweight Windows: New & Selected Poems, Donald Revell
Matadora, Sarah Gambito
In the Ghost-House Acquainted, Kevin Goodan
The Devotion Field, Claudia Keelan

ALICE JAMES BOOKS has been publishing poetry since 1973 and remains one of the few presses in the country that is run collectively. The cooperative selects manuscripts for publication primarily through regional and national annual competitions. Authors who win a Kinereth Gensler Award become active members of the cooperative board and participate in the editorial decisions of the press. The press, which historically has placed an emphasis on publishing women poets, was named for Alice James, sister of William and Henry, whose fine journal and gift for writing went unrecognized during her lifetime.

Typeset and Designed by Christopher Kuntze

Printed by Thomson-Shore
on 30% postconsumer recycled paper
processed chlorine-free